C000245295

THE *HEYDAY* OF
CROSVILLE

Martin Jenkins and Charles Roberts

Ian Allan
PUBLISHING

Front cover: Recorded in July 1964 by student conductor Bryan Pyne, this scene encapsulates the heyday of Crosville. It features the family on holiday, the Odeon, and a sparkling open-platform, half-cab double-decker swinging onto Rhyl station forecourt, which in the summer months served as an overspill bus station. Bristol K6A/ECW DKA372 looks set to carry another full load of holidaymakers to one of the myriad coastal camp sites to the west of the town. Earlier in its life (as MB372) loaned to London Transport, this veteran would eventually be withdrawn in 1966. Today the cinema is a listed building. *B. D. Pyne*

Back cover: Many Crosville routes were rural in nature, some being introduced in the 1960s as rail-replacement services. Following secondary roads on the east side of the Dee Valley, the D94 paralleled the ex-GWR line between Corwen and Bala. Here dual-purpose Bristol RESL/ ECW ERG5 crosses the 18th-century bridge spanning the River Ceidiog at Llandrillo, a typical Welsh village with its whitewashed cottages and one-time railway station. The shorter (31ft) 42-seat Bristol RESLs were ideally suited to this kind of territory, where many roads were still unsuitable for larger vehicles. When delivered in 1967 ERG5 had been painted cream with a green waistband, in common with the rest of the batch (ERG1-6); following withdrawal in 1980 most would go for scrap, but ERG3 was to see further use with a Wrexham-based scout troop and survives today in preservation. *D. Kerrison*

Previous page: The first cross-Wirral service, connecting New Ferry with West Kirby, commenced in 1919. Over the years a variety of routes linked New Ferry with the west side of the peninsula, among them the F42 (Heswall via Brimstage). Overlooked by the Three Stags public house, DFB49 turns at Spital Cross Roads, Bebington, on 8 September 1967. Between 1953 and 1968 Crosville received almost 600 Lodekkas, which came in many different guises and with a mix of engine types; DFB49, in service from 1961 until 1976, was one of the first of 84 30ft FLF (Flat floor, Long wheelbase, Forward entrance) models delivered 1961-8. *A. E. Jones*

First published 2009

ISBN (13) 978 0 7110 3401 3

All rights reserved. No part of this book may be reproduced or transmitted in any form or by any means, electronic or mechanical, including photocopying, recording or by any information storage and retrieval system, without permission from the Publisher in writing.

© Ian Allan Publishing 2009

Published by Ian Allan Publishing

an imprint of Ian Allan Publishing Ltd, Hersham, Surrey, KT12 4RG.
Printed in England by Ian Allan Printing Ltd, Hersham, Surrey, KT12 4RG.

Code: 0910/B

Visit the Ian Allan Publishing website at www.ianallanpublishing.com

Below: During the period covered by this book Rock Ferry was the largest and most important Wirral depot. Opened in 1932, the 'state-of-the-art' building had a spacious interior and a large maintenance facility. Later a large yard was provided to accommodate approximately 90 buses. Conveniently located on the Birkenhead–Chester artery, the depot's forecourt was used as a boarding-point for coach services. This elevated view, recorded in 1966 by Glynn Parry, a one-time conductor at Rock Ferry, features among the parked vehicles numerous Bristol Lodekkas and a couple of highbridge Ks and also illustrates the depot's proximity to the River Mersey, where a BP tanker, its funnel flanked by Liverpool's two cathedrals, can be seen tied up at the Tranmere oil jetty. *G. D. Parry*

Introduction

The name Crosland-Taylor will forever be synonymous with Crosville. George Crosland-Taylor was the joint founder of the company and its first Chairman, from 1906 to 1923. His second son, Claude, served as Chairman from 1923 to 1929 and thereafter until 1935 as Managing Director, a post then held by his brother, James (known as 'W. J.'), until 1959. Despite several changes of ownership Crosville managed to retain the feel of a family firm, much of its workforce staying with the company for many years.

So how did it all start? In May 1906 **Cros**land-Taylor Senior had teamed up with French designer and engineer Georges **Ville** to found the Crosville Motor Co Ltd, with the aim of manufacturing marine engines and high-quality motor cars at Crane Wharf, Chester. This collaboration produced just five cars, of which three were actually built in France. In 1911, to supplement his engineering business, Crosland-Taylor started a bus service between Chester and Ellesmere Port, soon followed by another, linking Chester and New Ferry, Birkenhead. During World War 1 new bus routes were established around Crewe and Nantwich, while from 1912 until 1919 additional income was derived from road haulage.

After the war rapid expansion saw Crosville serving parts of industrial North Wales and much of the Wirral Peninsula, as well as establishing a presence in Liverpool, Runcorn, Warrington and Crewe. By 1926 it had developed an extensive network, albeit one with many gaps, notably in much of North Wales, including Anglesey, as well as the more industrial area around Wrexham. In the late 1920s additional revenue came from 'luxurious express coach services', which eventually provided links to London, Blackpool and the North Wales coastal resorts. Introduced in 1928, Crosville's 'Conducted Coach Tours' were promoted as 'amongst the finest holidays available in the Kingdom'.

By 1929 the bus fleet had grown to approximately 300 and had adopted a grey livery. In that year the company was sold to the London, Midland & Scottish Railway, which replaced the grey livery with its own maroon and changed the fleetname to 'LMS (Crosville)', Crosland-Taylor being retained as General Manager. The following year the LMS sold half of its interest to the Tilling & British Automobile Traction Co Ltd (T&BAT), the company now being reformed as Crosville Motor Services Ltd but with the Crosland-Taylor family still having a relatively free hand.

From the very beginning the company had pursued a policy of buying out competitors, so that by the mid-1920s the Crosville empire stretched over a huge area. The Road Traffic Act 1930 accelerated consolidation of ownership in the industry, and in the early 1930s Crosville took advantage by acquiring three major independent companies in North Wales. Then, in 1933, Crosville became the key player in the Wrexham area, having acquired the Western Transport Co. By the outbreak of war in 1939 Crosville had a fleet of well over 1,000 vehicles, making it one of the largest bus operators in the country. However, plans for coach tours of Germany had been halted abruptly in 1938, and the programme of fully inclusive tours was suspended in September 1939, never to be reinstated.

World War 2 brought many challenges. The industrial areas of Merseyside were targets for air raids and both Rock Ferry (Birkenhead) and Edge Lane (Liverpool) depots suffered damage. Many express services were suspended for the duration, but in contrast, additional services had to be laid on for essential wartime work, most notably in Wrexham, where other operators' buses were received on long-term loan to supplement the fleet. During the war the company passed from T&BAT to the Tilling Group, which then sold out to the newly formed British Transport Commission in 1947. As a result the bus livery changed from LMS maroon to Tilling green.

Crosville's early bus fleet had been extremely varied, batches of Daimlers, Crossleys and Leylands contrasting with small numbers of marques such as Lacre and Tilling-Stevens. For new purchases the company standardised on Leylands from 1922 onwards, but every business taken over brought with it different types, some of which remained in the fleet for many years. Until 1939 single-deckers or 'saloons' accounted for 85% of the fleet. The first double-deckers (a batch of Leyland Leviathans) entered the fleet in 1926, and thereafter small numbers were allocated mostly to the Crewe and Merseyside depots. World War 2 brought deliveries of Leyland, Guy and Bristol double-deckers to serve labour-intensive factories.

Two other members of the state-owned Tilling Group were Bristol Commercial Vehicles and Eastern Coach Works (ECW). From 1947 until the early 1970s Crosville was obliged to standardise on these two companies for chassis and bodywork, although in the immediate postwar era, when new vehicles were in short supply, relatively small numbers of other makes were acquired. The company's engineering staff also worked hard to overcome these shortages. Between 1946 and 1953 many older chassis received new bodies, other bodies were extensively rebuilt, and modern designs of diesel engine replaced older petrol engines.

By the summer of 1954 the company was operating some 1,300 vehicles from 45 depots and sub-depots (some with only a single bus), but by now the decline had already set in. After carrying its greatest number of passengers — more than 193,000,000 — in the year ending 31 December 1949, Crosville experienced a steady fall in ridership. Just as operating costs, including wages, were beginning to increase, the rapid growth in car ownership, the advent of television and the end of the 5½-day working week were leading to significant reductions in revenue, and management now questioned the viability of many of the company's rural operations, especially in Wales. For decades the profitable Merseyside routes had effectively subsidised uneconomic operations in rural Cheshire, Shropshire and Wales — in the early 1950s the Birkenhead–Ellesmere Port–Chester group of routes alone accounted for 11% of total revenue — but this situation was felt to be unsustainable in the longer term.

The 1960s were marked by declining revenue, falling patronage, labour shortages and increasing congestion. Like much of the UK bus industry Crosville was in something of a parlous state. Starting in the mid-1960s, the policy was to axe unremunerative routes, reduce frequencies and acquire high-capacity one-man single-deckers. Despite this 60% of the fleet remained crew-operated double-deckers until the middle of the decade. By 1969 the fleet totalled just over 1,000 vehicles.

The 1963 reorganisation of the state-owned transport industry saw Crosville placed under the control of the Transport Holding Co, and then, from 1969, of the National Bus Company (NBC). The most visible sign of this latter was the change of livery to the less-well-loved 'leaf green', at first with no relief colour at all. Initially Crosville expanded, reorganisation within NBC bringing into its ownership certain former North Western depots. But on a like-for-like basis the fleet got smaller every year, and depots continued to close. Operationally the biggest changes were in the Merseyside area, where Crosville and the newly formed Passenger Transport Executive (PTE) reached agreement to create an integrated network, which ended the picking-up and setting-down restrictions in Birkenhead, Wallasey and Liverpool.

The radical Transport Act 1985 heralded the prospect of private ownership along with a reversion to pre-1931-style on-the-road competition. And there was a sting in the tail for Crosville. It was decreed by the Secretary of State for Transport that the company was too large to be sold as a single entity, so, with effect from 10 August 1986, operations from Welsh depots (plus Oswestry) were transferred to a new company, Crosville Wales Ltd. The privatisation of Crosville Motor Services Ltd was an unhappy affair, and the company was finally wound up on 30 March 1990, its assets having been dispersed to several different owners. Industry consolidation has, ironically, brought much of its former vast empire into Arriva ownership, but the Crosville name has gone, along with so much that once characterised this great company.

***

Everyone will have his or her own idea about what constitutes Crosville's heyday, and indeed this book's two authors have very different memories.

'We were evacuated to Rhyl, and I remember during the blackout waving down big red buses with a pencil-thin torch. Subsequently, in the immediate postwar years, I was fascinated by the extraordinary variety of vehicles, mostly Leylands but also including AECs, Bedfords and Guys. Particular favourites were the delightful N-class Cubs. I recall one exciting ride into the wilds during the 1947 school summer holidays, part of which we spent at Betws-y-Coed. On another occasion, possibly also in 1947, having queued for hours, my mother and I stood all the way back from Chester to Birkenhead on the staircase of an elderly Titan. Arriving at Woodside, we found that all buses on the jointly operated Birkenhead/Wallasey route 10 were packed, so we trudged home across the Dock Estate to New Brighton. On a return visit to Rhyl during the summer of 1948 we enjoyed a leisurely ride on a "toast-rack"; some years later we repeated the trip, but this time on an E-class 'boat' which I recall watching in amazement as it drew up on the promenade. The routes I used the most were the 1 (Birkenhead–Chester) and the 106 (Wallasey–West Kirby); my personal favourites were the 101 (Birkenhead–Loggerheads), 105 (Birkenhead–Meols) and 412 (Llandudno–Betws-y-Coed). In my teens I also spent many hours exploring Crosville's nooks and crannies, including (often unofficially) depots such as Rock Ferry and West Kirby but above all Wrexham, where the yard was a veritable treasure-trove of oddities and one-offs. But the Crosville I knew and loved lost much of its variety and individuality during the 1950s.' *(M. J.)*

'By contrast, my earliest recollections of Crosville are deeply rooted in the Bristol/ECW era of the 1960s. I have a few memories of the sunken-gangway, lowbridge Bristol KSWs which contrasted greatly with the municipal fleets of Birkenhead and Wallasey and their highbridge Leylands and Guys. When we had days out and holidays as a family Crosville's empire was so large that it was not unusual to find its buses at our destination. The open-top Lodekkas at Rhyl and Prestatyn bore a similarity to those I was used to back home — body squeaks and all — but wore an attractive cream and black livery, and of course had no roof. I was always intrigued by the "Publications" page in the Crosville timetable. A "Crosville Fleet List … A must for all bus enthusiasts" was something I felt I should have, even at the age of eight, so, on a day trip to Chester (no doubt on the C1 — successor to the 1 which Martin remembers), I persuaded my dad to take me to that mythical place, "Publicity Dept, Crosville, Crane Wharf, Chester", where he bought me the book for 4s 6d [22½p in today's money]. I still have it, of course.

The F34 — Wallasey (Liscard)–West Kirby–Birkenhead (Park Station) — and its short-journey variants got me to and from school through the 1970s, with its slowly modernising fleet and its familiar drivers and conductors. And Crosville even provided me with my first job — Technical Assistant (Temporary) at Sealand Road Works — while I was a student in the late 1970s. By that time the company was well past its heyday, and it's been sad to see what's happened to it since, but I still take a certain pride in being able to say that I worked for a company with a history as illustrious as Crosville's.' *(C. R.)*

***

Dating from the period 1954-73, the images in this book have been selected to feature as many vehicle types as possible in a wide variety of locations, following a broadly geographical sequence starting from and returning to Chester, the company's spiritual home. But, before we start, a few words of explanation.

Fleet numbers
Originally Crosville used a purely numerical system for its vehicles, many numbers being used more than once over the years. In 1933 an alphabetical classification system was introduced, initially with just a single letter prefix. For example, 'A' denoted a short-wheelbase Leyland PLSC1, while 'U' covered a collection of miscellaneous types, including the Shelvoke & Drewry 'toast racks' (as illustrated on page 41). Postwar, two-letter classifications were used to identify certain sub-types, the prewar Tiger shown on page 9 being originally classified 'K' but redesignated 'KC' when re-engined. From 1958 a three-letter prefix was introduced, the three characters representing body, chassis and engine type; for example, a 'DLG' was a **D**ouble-deck Bristol **L**D with a **G**ardner engine. Many older types, nearing withdrawal, were excluded from this new system. In this book we have generally used the code in use at the time the picture was taken.

Route numbers
Under pressure from Tilling, Crosville introduced a route-numbering system in 1946. However, as it was rather muddled, with much duplication, passengers often relied on the route information carried on the 'Widd' plates displayed in the nearside bulkhead window. In 1959 this system was replaced by one of area prefixes, an 'A' series being used by Flint and Holywell, 'C' by the Chester area etc. From 1964 an 'L' series was reserved for limited-stop services, while 'X' denoted 'Express'.

Place names
The greater part of Crosville's operating territory was in Wales. The authors have used today's spellings throughout, even though these are sometimes at odds with the spellings on destination blinds or on signage. Hence 'Caernarfon' is used in preference to 'Caernarvon', and 'Betws-y-Coed' to the many alternatives — 'Bettws-y-Coed', 'Bettys-y-Coed' etc — that have appeared over the years.

Acknowledgements
The authors would like to express their gratitude to everyone who has contributed photographs. Particular thanks are due to Steve Williams for access to the Mike Cozens collection, to Richard Morant for access to the Geoffrey Morant collection, to Eileen Tatt for access to the Philip Tatt collection and to Mair and Andy McCann for access to the John McCann collection. Significant help in checking caption details has been given by Bill Barlow, Dennis Kerrison, Bruce Maund and Steve Williams, while Glynn Parry and Geoff Smith have provided insights into their time spent working for Crosville. The authors would also like to thank Peter Thompson and Dr and Mrs Swigg. Like the authors' previous volume, *Streets of Liverpool* (Ian Allan, 2007), this book has been compiled in conjunction with Online Transport Archive (OTA), a charity ensuring the preservation for posterity of photographs and moving images of transport, and to which the authors' fees have been donated.

Bibliography
In the course of their research the authors have drawn on a number of publications, most notably *The Sowing and the Harvest* and *State-Owned Without Tears* by W. J. Crosland-Taylor (Littlebury Bros, Liverpool, 1948 and 1953), *History of Crosville Motor Services* by R. C. Anderson (David & Charles, 1981), *Crosville on Merseyside* by T. B. Maund (TPC, 1992), *Crosville Motor Services — the First 40 Years* by John Carroll and Duncan Roberts (Venture Publications, 1995) and *Crosville Motor Services 2* by Duncan Roberts (NBC Books, 1997). Much vehicle information has come from the series of 'Crosville Handbooks' published annually by the company throughout the 1950s, from Ian Allan's 'ABCs' and from the comprehensive three-part 'Fleet History' published jointly by the PSV Circle and The Omnibus Society.

Martin Jenkins   *Charles Roberts*
Walton-on-Thames, Surrey   Upton, Wirral
August 2009

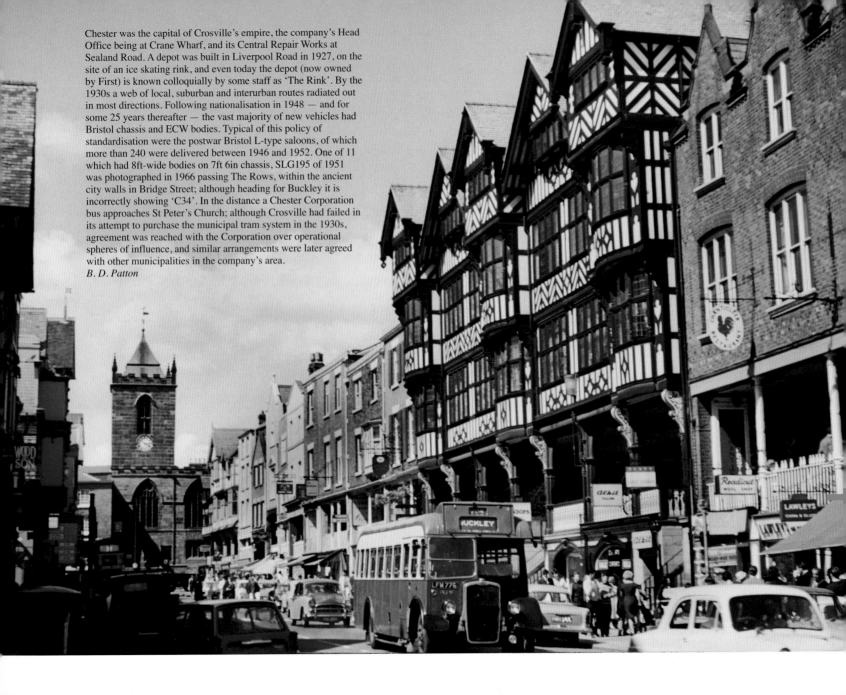

Chester was the capital of Crosville's empire, the company's Head Office being at Crane Wharf, and its Central Repair Works at Sealand Road. A depot was built in Liverpool Road in 1927, on the site of an ice skating rink, and even today the depot (now owned by First) is known colloquially by some staff as 'The Rink'. By the 1930s a web of local, suburban and interurban routes radiated out in most directions. Following nationalisation in 1948 — and for some 25 years thereafter — the vast majority of new vehicles had Bristol chassis and ECW bodies. Typical of this policy of standardisation were the postwar Bristol L-type saloons, of which more than 240 were delivered between 1946 and 1952. One of 11 which had 8ft-wide bodies on 7ft 6in chassis, SLG195 of 1951 was photographed in 1966 passing The Rows, within the ancient city walls in Bridge Street; although heading for Buckley it is incorrectly showing 'C34'. In the distance a Chester Corporation bus approaches St Peter's Church; although Crosville had failed in its attempt to purchase the municipal tram system in the 1930s, agreement was reached with the Corporation over operational spheres of influence, and similar arrangements were later agreed with other municipalities in the company's area.

B. D. Patton

Above: Crosville's two prime objectives in its expanding Wirral-based network were access to either the cross-Mersey ferries or the under-river Mersey Railway and to entice people 'from over the water' to use their services. The first objective was achieved in stages, Crosville finally reaching the Woodside transport hub in 1930, whilst the second eventually had thousands crossing over to board buses for the Wirral and North Wales. Despite gaining access to Woodside, the company was subjected to restrictions with regard to picking up and setting down within the boundaries of Birkenhead and Bebington. On arrival buses off-loaded outside the ferry building (1864), but departures were from queueing points along the north side of the railway station (1878), which, until its closure in 1967, offered an alternative means of travel to many destinations. Although still using the ferry approach, after

1948 Crosville concentrated on connections with the newly nationalised rail network. Waiting to depart for Heswall on the F19 was DKB633, one of 87 55-seat lowbridge KSW6Bs delivered during 1952/3. This final development of the standard K differed from earlier versions through being 8ft wide and 27ft long, having a stepped front cab and having four (as opposed to five) windows between the lower saloon bulkheads. Former conductor Glynn Parry referred to the DKBs as 'mobile cold-storage units' and recalls that, during the winter, condensation created by upper-deck passengers would freeze on the ceilings, so that in the mornings all bell-pushes had to checked to ensure they had not frozen up. DKB633 would be withdrawn shortly after this photograph was taken in 1967. *Peter Jackson*

Left: Although during the 1960s the fleet was characterised by uniformity, replacement being generally on a like-for-like basis, there were occasional exceptions. Among these were 12 Bristol MWs loaned from Red & White for a 12-month period in 1967/8, during which time they retained their Red & White fleet numbers but were repainted in Crosville green. Dating from 1958/9, they had been needed to increase the availability of one-man-operated (OMO) vehicles. No U2359 (VWO 233) was recorded working the F27 on 10 April 1968, by which date Woodside station (right) was awaiting demolition; in the background, across the Mersey, can be seen Liverpool's imposing Liver Building. Paradoxically, at the conclusion of the loan, the MWs were replaced by a batch of older Red & White Bristol LSs which were purchased outright, as illustrated on page 35. *J. M. Ryan*

Below left: To offer a quicker journey along some trunk corridors, several limited-stop services were introduced. Offering a 10min saving between Birkenhead and Chester, the Saturdays-only L5 first began operation in March 1969. At Woodside Ferry on 13 June 1970 a gent consults his watch as he hurries towards one of many Bristol RE saloons (with rear-mounted underfloor engines) delivered between 1967 and 1971; these came with a variety of body styles, SRG175, a 53-seat single-door bus new in April 1970, being one of the last delivered with a flat windscreen. For many years this was generally the stopping point for Liverpool-bound expresses, and across the road a Bristol MW coach offloads outside the Woodside Hotel. The tall building beyond is one of the ventilator shafts for the Mersey Tunnel, while in the background (right) can again be seen the Liver Building. Today Woodside Ferry has a much smaller (and much less well-used) bus station, but it also has a heritage tramway and has recently become home to a World War 2 German U-boat sectioned for display. The Woodside Hotel, which until the 1970s had a Crosville office attached, was demolished after being damaged by fire in 2008. *D. Kerrison*

Heswall was transformed into a prosperous town by the coming of the railway in 1886, while the combined depot and bus station built by Crosville in 1924 (and from 1930 used also by Birkenhead Corporation) was probably the first purpose-built example in the North of England. On 27 May 1961 an F19 has just arrived from Birkenhead. Some of its passengers are walking away, whilst others would have transferred onto the F25 shuttle to Banks Road, one of the last Wirral routes to be operated by half-cab saloons. In the foreground Bristol FLF DFB51 is turning into Telegraph Road at the start of its 27min journey to Woodside via Pensby. Typifying the intensity of many of Crosville's major Wirral routes, the F19 ran mostly every 15 minutes, increasing in frequency to every 10 minutes and, for a brief spell, every 5 minutes during rush hours; there was also a 10min headway on Saturday afternoons, to cater for the crowds going over 'to town' (Liverpool) to shop or to attend football matches or places of entertainment. Between Heswall and Thingwall Corner combined bus and ferry tickets were available, and these were also accepted on Birkenhead Corporation buses. Heswall depot closed in 1988, and, after an attempt by Crosville's new owners to sell off the entire site for redevelopment, a compromise was reached, and a smaller, modern bus station built by Merseytravel. The pub occupying the former depot yard is called the 'Johnny Pye', after the proprietor of the Heswall-based bus company bought out by Crosville in 1924.
D. Kerrison

9

Located on the north-west tip of the Wirral peninsula, West Kirby was another Crosville hub complete with depot (1923). This small town, with its elegant shops, impressive villas, marine lake and promenade, exuded an air of genteel prosperity. On fine days people came by bus and train to sample the sea-breezes and the views across the Dee Estuary, while for several years a nearby RAF camp generated much additional traffic. Busier services demanded double-deckers, but saloons sufficed for more 'rural' routes, like the F27 (Meols–West Kirby–Irby Mill Hill–Woodside). Seen loading in Banks Road in the late 1960s is SMG444 of 1963, one of 103 Bristol MW (Medium Weight) single-deckers delivered between 1959 and 1966. Equipped for OMO, this example had a 41-seat body, fluorescent lighting and the Cave-Browne-Cave heating and ventilation system, not to mention some recently sustained accident damage. Crosville prided itself on its facilities for staff, and West Kirby was home to one of many employees' social clubs. Even today, nearly 20 years after the demise of the company name, the Crosville Club in Grange Road remains open for business. *Peter Jackson*

Back in Birkenhead, another terminus was established in 1924 in Beckwith Street, close to Park station, with connections onto Mersey Railway trains into Liverpool. In the 1930s arrangements were reorganised to include loading stands, a waiting room and an inspector's hut built on land owned by the railway. In peak hours buses frequently double-parked, engines running, waiting for the next train-load of commuters. To maximise the life of its fleet Crosville often downgraded older vehicles. DLB682 started life in 1954 as one of eight semi-luxury Lodekkas designed for express work and painted in a livery of all over cream, but by the late 1960s, after a interim period in green and cream (see page 70), all eight were in green bus livery and largely confined to local work. Redolent of a more luxurious era are the scalloped-back seats, a chrome band between the decks and a straight staircase to allow for more luggage space. In the background can be seen two Birkenhead Corporation vehicles, a Massey-bodied Leyland PD2 on route 42 turning into Duke Street and catching up with a 1964 Daimler Fleetline on route 21. A short walk to the left led to the once labour-intensive Birkenhead Docks. *Peter Jackson*

Left: Wartime shortages and strictures reinforced Crosville's established policy of gaining the maximum life from its fleet, as will be apparent from the first of three photographs featuring elderly Leylands formerly in the company's employ. For decades the Mersey docks housed a variety of pensioned-off buses, and noted on the Birkenhead side during an Omnibus Society trip on 21 April 1968 was one of more than 350 Lions received by Crosville between 1926 and 1930. Although its PLSC1 chassis dated from 1927, FM 4287 (original fleet number 251, later A17) had received a new Eastern Counties body in 1936. Acquired by A. E. Smith Coggins of Liverpool in 1949, it was used as an office, rest room and canteen for dock labourers. *Peter Roberts*

Below left: A Tiger TS2 new in 1930, FM 5898 (numbered successively 350, K23 and KC23 in the Crosville fleet) had its original coach body replaced in the mid-1930s by a 32-seat dual-purpose ECW body, while during the war it hauled a gas-producing trailer and was also fitted with perimeter seating. It escaped the late-1940s cull of prewar vehicles because it had been given a Gardner diesel engine; finally withdrawn and sold in 1956, it appears to have been working for a contractor when photographed, several years later, at the Birkenhead end of the Queensway road tunnel. *J. N. Barlow / Online Transport Archive*

Below: The former J10 (FM 8980), a Lion LT7 of 1935, which was reclassified as JG10 in 1949 when it received a new Gardner engine and replacement ECW body. Withdrawn by Crosville in 1959, it then served with a stevedoring company. Sadly none of these veterans was rescued for preservation. *Chris Moyes / Online Transport Archive*

Crosville eventually reached Liverpool's Pier Head in 1932, a series of exposed loading points being established on the east side of this large windswept terminal, which eventually became the starting point for a network of heavily used express, inter-urban, suburban and urban routes. This view, recorded in 1956, features two of the world-famous waterfront buildings — the Liver Building (1911) and the Cunard Building (1914). The Crosville Bristol K (right) is working one of the many variations of route 116, whilst the Lodekka behind, still with its upper-deck cream band, is on the 119 to Warrington. Both have three-piece destination displays; note, however, that at this time the final destination was sometimes shown in the lower (as opposed to the upper) aperture. On the left of the picture is a Liverpool Corporation four-wheel 'Baby Grand' tram bound for Bowring Park, while in the background can be seen a variety of Corporation buses and the cranes of the northern docks. Liverpool's last trams would disappear in 1957. *D. Norman / Online Transport Archive*

Left: Following wartime suspension the Liverpool–North Wales express services were gradually restored. To cope with the crowds wanting to visit resorts such as Rhyl and Llandudno, especially at weekends, scores of duplicates were usually needed. Some North Wales depots despatched fully crewed empty buses, whilst other vehicles were hired, usually with drivers, from the Merseyside municipalities, principally Liverpool Corporation. In this view, recorded at Pier Head during the summer of 1956, L97, a Duple-bodied Leyland PD2, carries an 'on hire to Crosville' sticker and displays route number 127, this being Crosville's trunk coastal express service. Alongside, providing the 16th duplicate on the service, probably as far as Rhyl, is Wallasey Corporation 103, a Burlingham-bodied PD2. Among the range of fares and excursions was an outward trip from the Pier Head by Liverpool & North Wales steamship and a return by coach, for which advance tickets could be purchased at Crosville's Edge Lane depot or from an office located in Liverpool's premier 'Welsh' store, Owen Owen. *J. B. C. McCann*

Above: Opened in 1928, the depot in Edge Lane, one of the company's largest, eventually required a high proportion of double-deckers for the Liverpool-area services, many of which paralleled Corporation routes within the city boundary. The complex also served as the starting point for a number of well-patronised express services, including the premier X1 (Liverpool–London), with its roster of top drivers, and the many North Wales expresses, and after making additional pick-ups in the city centre such coaches used the under-river Queensway road tunnel to arrive at further stopping points on the Wirral. On 9 September 1972 CMG430 was bound for Tywyn on a short working of the X3 Caernarfon service. Dating from 1962, this 39-seat coach had the later style of MW body featuring stepped waistline, wraparound corner windows, fluorescent lighting and the Cave-Browne-Cave heating system, although its original curved rooflights had been replaced by fibreglass panels in the mid-1960s. All the 1962 MW coaches were downgraded and reclassified as EMG in the early 1970s after being fitted for OMO, with driver-operated doors. *A. Drury*

Left: The principal Crosville exit from central Liverpool was by way of Wavertree Road and Picton Road to Wavertree Clock Tower, where the Widnes and Huyton services diverged. Seen inbound in Wavertree Road on 21 March 1972, with reduced destination display and in-house advertising for the company's coach services, is Lodekka DLG791; new in 1956 as MG791, it had originally had a partially enclosed platform but was only subsequently fitted with doors. Served by trams until 1949, this part of Wavertree Road, with its three-storey yellow-brick properties, was close to Edge Hill railway station. The H9 was an industrial service which by the early 1970s made a few weekday trips between Prescot and Pier Head and additional workpeople's journeys to the Huntley & Palmer factory at Huyton. Despite an agreement between Crosville and Merseyside Passenger Transport Executive, aimed at eliminating crew operation, Lodekkas would survive in the Liverpool area until 1981, but DLG791 bowed out in 1975. *A. Drury*

Right: Although Crosville was generally averse to joint working, certain complex agreements meant that it did participate in such services as the 89, operated jointly with St Helens Corporation. Although numbered in the Liverpool series this route was never operated by the Corporation or by Ribble Motor Services, which until 1985 owned an 8% share. Adding to the confusion, it was shown as the 137 in Crosville timetables, which also persisted in referring to Woolton (Tram Terminus) long after the trams had gone. Seen in St Helens at the start of its run to Speke is DFG244. A Bristol FLF new in 1967, this was one of a final batch of 12 half-cabs which, unlike all other Crosville Lodekkas, were equipped with semi-automatic transmission rather than the more common crash gearbox. These late Lodekkas also had the Clayton heating system, which obviated the need for the grilles on either side of the destination display. *A. F. Gahan*

Right: Neither the 89 nor the 140 were given the 'H' prefix applied to routes operating from Liverpool and Warrington depots as part of the 1959 route renumbering. Crosville's share of the 140, a tripartite operation with St Helens and Warrington corporations, was provided by Warrington depot. On 27 March 1969, shortly before the 140's conversion to OMO, Bristol MW SMG374 approaches Warrington Arpley bus station. The early ECW bus body for the MW featured inward-facing seats over the front wheel arches. *Alan Murray-Rust*

The absence of a major road bridge over the Mersey in the Runcorn/Widnes area forced Crosville to develop unconnected networks on either side of the river. Since 1926 some services had used the impressive but antiquated Runcorn Transporter Bridge (1905); when this was replaced by a high-level road bridge, on 21 July 1961, new through Liverpool–Runcorn–Chester routes (H20-24) were introduced the same evening, to be followed four days later by workmen's service H25, which on weekdays and Saturdays linked Liverpool with Runcorn via the Speke Industrial Estate. Showing the smaller fleetname introduced in 1966, Lodekka DLG799 of 1955 waits in Speke Hall Avenue to pick up workers from the large Dunlop factory. Today long-stay car parks occupy the factory site, and the road has been incorporated into a dual-carriageway leading to the terminal building at Liverpool's John Lennon Airport. *Peter Jackson*

Right: In 1964 designated by the Government as a New Town, the port of Runcorn was transformed during the 1960s and 1970s, and introduced to coincide with the opening of Shopping City on 1 November 1971 were new services J61-63, operated jointly by Crosville and Widnes Corporation. Pictured outside the Black Horse at Farnworth, northern terminus of the J63, is Bristol RELL SRG135. Crosville's standard single-decker of the period, the RE/ECW saloon came in two different lengths, in single- and dual-door configuration and with various styles of frontal design; new in 1969, SRG135 was a dual-door, long-wheelbase vehicle with a flat front and deep windscreen, and was destined to remain in service until the early 1980s. *Peter Jackson*

Below right: Central to the concept of Runcorn as a New Town was a system of segregated public transport providing a fast link between the old town, the railway station and the New Town's vast areas of housing. Opened in stages between 1971 and 1978, the Runcorn Busway comprised a 12-mile figure of eight with traffic lights that gave priority to buses. Designed for use by single-deckers, the 22ft-wide track allowed for a top speed of 40mph. Eventually operated from a new depot adjacent to the busway, routes using the network were given the hitherto unused 'T' prefix. Photographed when brand-new on 14 October 1971, the day the first seven-mile section opened, SPG776 was one of 100 rear-engined Seddon Pennine RUs (comprising 50 dual-door saloons and 50 single-door dual-purpose vehicles, the latter designated 'EPG') delivered to Crosville in 1971/2. They were never a great success, withdrawals beginning in 1980, and most donated their engines and gearboxes to Leyland Nationals before being sold for scrap. *Peter Jackson*

Some 20 miles south-east of Runcorn is Crewe. Although Crosville had been purchased by the LMS in 1929 there was opposition to bus expansion from local town councillors, many of whom were railwaymen, and this effectively prevented Crosville from securing a monopoly of town services until 1934. After much delay a new bus station with adjacent depot and divisional offices opened on 21 June 1960.

Departing on town service K24 is DLB687, an early Lodekka. When this photograph was taken on 5 October 1967 it retained its 'long apron' design of radiator grille, but the destination display has been reconfigured to show just route number and destination, the upper aperture having been painted over. *W. Ryan*

This page: Located just outside the town (and nowadays surrounded by industrial sprawl), Crewe Hall is an imposing early-17th-century Jacobean mansion, gutted by fire in 1866 and rebuilt with an additional wing and a lofty tower. Used during World War 2 to house Australian and American soldiers and later as a prisoner-of-war camp for German officers, it served subsequently as the headquarters and research and manufacturing base of pharmaceutical firm CALMIC (Cheshire and Lancashire Medical Industries Corporation). Although not listed in the public timetable, a couple of scheduled works services provided transport for fare-paying employees, and these two photographs were taken in 1969, shortly before the services were discontinued. In the first, Lodekka DLB22 of 1960 exits through the imposing gates on the 16.30 K27 departure to Crewe on a snowy St Valentine's Day, when the Cave-Browne-Cave heating and cooling system would doubtless have been welcome. The second view, recorded in more clement conditions on 5 April, features a pair of Lodekkas, that nearer the camera being DLB770 of 1955. Today the Grade I-listed Hall is a luxury hotel. *W. Ryan*

Dating from 1920, the Chester–Crewe–Newcastle-under-Lyme service was a classic Crosville inter-urban route, total journey time in the late 1960s being approximately 1 hour 45 minutes. Seen waiting in the High Street in the centre of Newcastle on 13 April 1968 is DFB132 of 1963, one of the company's numerous 60-seat, rear-entrance FS-type Lodekkas. In the background (left) stands the imposing Guildhall (1713), while beyond the bus can be seen the Rex and Rio cinemas, which had been taken over by the Essoldo group and would be demolished after closure in 1973. Many of the other buildings still survive, although the High Street is now a pedestrian precinct. Latterly one of the last Bristol-engined vehicles to remain in the fleet, DFB132 would be sold in 1980. *W. Ryan*

We now return to the hub at Chester, where the web of routes included 'locals' such as the C46 from Blacon to Plas Newton estate. Turning from Hunter Street into Northgate Street on 5 April 1969 is DFG81, a Bristol FSF6G delivered in 1962. The combination of a flat-floor Lodekka with a short wheelbase and forward entrance was relatively rare; only 218 were built, of which Crosville had 30. One of a number decapitated in 1977 to revive open-top operation in Llandudno, DFG81 would be secured for preservation following withdrawal in 1984. Nowadays traffic travels along Hunter Street in the opposite direction, and at the time of writing the long-term future of the Grade II-listed Odeon cinema, built in 1936 but closed in 2007, remains in doubt. *W. Ryan*

23

One of several termini in Chester, Delamere Street was the boarding point for long-distance coach services such as the X1 to London. This was the company's premier express service, and during its heyday in the 1960s and early 1970s Edge Lane depot in Liverpool had a large roster of drivers assigned specifically to it. It was a two-day duty entailing an overnight stay in London, the total journey time in each direction (including a 30-minute lunch break and two 10-minute refreshment stops) being some 8 hours, and to meet peak demand other drivers could be reassigned from Liverpool's stage-carriage routes, leading to frustrating delays on local services.

Crosville's standard coach for flagship express services during most of the 1960s and 1970s was the Bristol RELH, a total of 76 being delivered between 1964 and 1975. Seen waiting to depart for the capital in 1968 are ECW-bodied CRG579 (new 1966) and CRG40 (new 1968). The side panels on the bodywork, which read 'CROSVILLE – LIVERPOOL – LONDON – EXPRESS', were illuminated at night. In 1972 a purpose-built bus and coach station was constructed across the road from these stops, and this was to serve as Crosville's main departure point throughout the NBC era. *A. Osborne*

Visitors arriving in London during the summer of 1958 encountered a prolonged bus strike, during which a skeleton service was provided by the People's League for the Defence of Freedom. Amongst the assembled fleet were several recently withdrawn Crosville Leyland TD7s, including the former M103. Diverted to the company in 1940 from East Kent, this was one of a batch of 10 (M101-10) which bore FN registrations (rather than the usual Chester FM), having been first licensed in Canterbury. Their original Park Royal lowbridge bodies, with sunken gangways upstairs, had been replaced in 1953 by new Crosville-built six-bay highbridge bodies, with unusual lower-saloon 'standee' windows. *J. Law / Online Transport Archive*

Farndon was one of many Crosville crossing points between England and Wales. This Cheshire village had been linked to Wrexham by Great Western Railway (GWR) buses as early as 1904 and to Chester by Crosville in 1915, and in the days when Wales was 'dry' on Sundays determined drinkers would frequent Farndon's pubs.

The village was also a starting point for leisurely river cruises to and from Chester. This delightful portrait from in 1968 depicts a Bristol L-series half-cab on the stone-arch bridge spanning the River Dee. For decades the more profitable English routes effectively subsidised Crosville's Welsh operations. *A. Moyes*

Right: Wrexham is the industrial and commercial capital of North Wales, although its traditional products — coal, steel, bricks, leather and ale — have given way to chemicals and textiles. After acquiring Western Transport in 1933 Crosville pursued a policy of buying out local independents, although quite a few survived. This photograph, taken in King Street on 25 April 1964, features a Bedford OB owned by George Edwards of Bwlchgwyn, who ran a single route to Llanarmon-yn-Lal from 1923 and still operates in the area today. Surrounding the OB are a selection of classic Crosville vehicles representing the Bristol/ECW combination characteristic of so many Tilling Group companies; nearest the camera is FLF Lodekka DFB117, with crew resting upstairs before departure on the trunk D2 to Oswestry. Since 1953 King Street had been Wrexham's principal bus station, in its heyday witnessing more than 1,000 departures daily. Plans for a grandiose terminal to be designed by renowned architect Giles Gilbert Scott never came to fruition. *G. Lumb*

Right: At King Street bus station on 12 April 1968 a mixed line of Lodekkas waits to enter the various numbered bays, each with its own concrete shelter. Reflecting the development of the Lodekka, all four vehicles have different features, and each appears in a different shade of green. Wrexham remained a bastion of crew-operated double-deckers until the early 1980s. For many years the depot, near the football ground in Mold Road, had Crosville's largest allocation, although many buses made only a few daily trips on industrial and school contract work. After the depot closed in 1991 the site was occupied by a housing estate. When King Street was redeveloped in 2003 it included a covered bus interchange. *J. M. Ryan*

Left: The evening exodus from Wrexham Industrial Estate, situated to the south-west of the town centre, included 'workpeople's services', many of which, together with various colliery, industrial and school services, had a 'G' prefix. Vehicles listed for sale often spent their final months assigned to these duties. For example, when photographed in March 1968, these were among the last of the K-type double-deckers in service. The vast majority of Crosville Ks were of the lowbridge, sunken-gangway type, but DKB440, pictured leading this convoy of vehicles, was one of just 15 delivered in 1952 with 60-seat highbridge bodies. Behind is DKB380, an older and more typical 55-seat lowbridge example of 1949. Reached by B roads, the estate occupied the site of the former wartime Marchwiel Royal Ordnance Factory, which, following its opening in 1940, employed a huge labour force, most arriving and departing by some 200 buses, many of which had been hired from other operators and were kept in the enormous open yard at Mold Road depot. The industrial estate, one of the largest in the country, was developed to provide much-needed work following the run-down of local industries. *Alan Mortimer*

Left: Situated four miles south-east of Wrexham is Johnstown, which from 1903 until 1927 was on the route of the narrow-gauge Wrexham & District Electric Tramways line. The former tram depot was occupied by Crosville following its takeover of Western Transport in 1933 and, as listed in Crosville timetables, had the memorable telephone number 'RHOS 9'. Pictured standing outside in March 1967 is CSG629, one of 24 Bristol SC coaches purchased between 1958 and 1960 as replacements for the Bedford OBs. Only 50 SC coaches were ever built, their low-powered Gardner 4LK engines hardly proving ideal for excursion work. Although retaining their coach classification these slow, noisy 33-seaters were downgraded in 1966 and fitted with automatic doors and new destination displays. In this guise they were mostly used at times of peak demand. One of Johnstown's duties was to cover shift-change workings between local collieries and surrounding villages such as Penycae. Scheduled to close in the late 1960s, this depot, with its cramped accommodation for around 20 vehicles, was finally vacated in May 1972 but not demolished until 2007. *A. Osborne*

Left: We now follow the course of the Dee westwards towards Corwen and Bala. Midway between Ruabon and Llangollen lies the village of Garth. When photographed in March 1968 SSG605 (formerly SC5) was covering a school-contract duty, a guaranteed source of much-needed income. This was one of Crosville's first batch of the saloon version of the SC, the first 20 being delivered during 1957/8 with forward-entrance 35-seat bodies. They were equipped for OMO from new, but, being front-engined, they required the driver to turn round to issue tickets over his shoulder. Purchased to maximise economies on loss-making services, these small-engined, lightweight vehicles were capable of achieving 20mpg. Following sale in early 1975 SSG605 would be one of a trio despatched to Orkney, but two other vehicles from this batch, SSG612/3, were destined to run for Crosville as heritage vehicles well into the privatised era. *Alan Mortimer*

Left: Since 1947 home to the International Eisteddfod, Llangollen is a major tourist centre. Until 1933 the inter-urban service to Chester via Wrexham had been operated by Western Transport. For much of the 1960s the D1 ran half-hourly on weekdays but with additional journeys between Wrexham and Chester, the full length taking just over 90 minutes. Seen outside the English Wesley Chapel (1857) in Market Street on 7 June 1970 is DFB179, another of the 60-seat, rear-loading FS-type Lodekkas. On delivery in 1965 it was painted with just a single cream band, although the bodywork still featured the moulding for an upper band. The next vehicle in the sequence (DFB180) was purchased for preservation in 1980 but currently remains in storage in as-withdrawn condition. *C. L. Caddy*

Above: The 10-mile scenic corridor between Llangollen and the small market town of Corwen had first been served by GWR buses. Following its takeover of Western Transport, Crosville built this small depot in 1934 in a space carved out of the hillside flanking London Road. Such buildings were typical of the cheaper structures erected by Crosville in less remunerative areas. Seen on 12 September 1971 are SMG587 and ERG1. Delivered in 1967, the latter was one of a batch of six Gardner-engined RESLs (Rear Engine, Short, Low frame) with dual-purpose bodywork. For many years these were associated with routes D93/94, introduced in 1965, as partial replacement for the former GWR Wrexham–Llangollen–Corwen–Barmouth rail service. During the 1960s large sections of the national rail network were closed, especially in much of rural Wales. Somewhat unwillingly, Crosville became involved in providing replacement bus services, which in most cases, despite some level of subsidy, proved yet another drain on resources. *D. Kerrison*

31

Dolgellau, some 30 miles south-west of Corwen, has long been a convenient base for exploring Snowdonia and was until the 1930s a centre for gold mining. Since 1963 Eldon Square had been the boarding point for express service 41 (Bangor–Cheltenham), which after 1965, when Crosville became a member of Associated Motorways, was operated jointly with the Bristol Omnibus Co. On arrival at Cheltenham passengers were able to transfer to virtually every point in the UK. When this view was recorded, on 18 June 1967, the 41 had been extended at the north end to Holyhead. Between 1958 and 1966 Crosville took delivery of 99 Bristol MW coaches, CMG561, being one of the final batch of 15. This particular design of ECW body, incorporating an RE-style grille, was unique to Crosville, while gone are the troublesome curved roof lights of early batches. Since withdrawal in 1980 CMG561 has had an interesting history: sold initially to a scout pack on the Wirral and thence to a fruit-picking concern in Scotland, it was acquired subsequently by Stagecoach as a source of spares for a member of its heritage fleet but was thankfully never used for this purpose, instead passing into preservation in 1999. *C. L. Caddy*

The Shropshire market town of Oswestry was the one-time headquarters of the Cambrian Railways and had an impressive station building, outside which SRG208 of 1970 was photographed when almost new. This was one of Crosville's last batch of Bristol RE saloons and featured a curved grille and windscreen. The latter was of the same type as that used by bodybuilders such as Marshall and Willowbrook on vehicles for the BET group and was less prone to night glare than the flat screen used on earlier REs. Crosville's Oswestry depot was situated across the road from the railway station and had come into company hands with the takeover of Western Transport. Although geographically in England, its operations were really part of the Welsh network, and it thus passed to Crosville Wales in 1986. The depot has since been demolished, but the station building survives. *Alan Snatt*

Left: Due south of Oswestry lies the market town of Welshpool. Pictured on the station forecourt on 21 June 1969 are two saloons on rail-replacement services. In 1965 the D71 was revised to provide partial replacement for the Whitchurch–Welshpool rail service, while the D85 was successor to the service which had replaced passenger trains on the Welshpool & Llanfair Light Railway (W&L) in 1931. After the W&L closed in 1956 this narrow-gauge railway was rescued by enthusiasts and gradually reopened. Working the D85, CUG296, was one of 37 semi-integral Bristol/ECW LS (Light Saloon) coaches with underfloor Gardner 8.4-litre engines and 39-seat bodies, dating from 1952/3. All had attractive corner glasses, and most had split windscreens, although a few were originally built with a roll-down type; subsequent alterations included the fitting of heaters, replacement of the awkward outward-facing door in 1960 with jack-knife doors and a bus-type front destination display. Converted for OMO in 1967, CUG296 was painted in dual-purpose livery, although retaining its coach classification. Behind, on the D71, can be seen SRG75, one of a batch of 30 RESL/ECW buses delivered in 1968/9. *Alan Murray-Rust*

Left: From 1970 Welshpool was served by the D75, a new Shrewsbury–Newtown service created after Crosville assumed responsibility for key routes formerly operated by Mid Wales Motorways. By the time this view was recorded on 25 May 1972 the route ran as far as Llanidloes. Covering this sparsely trafficked service is EMG356, one of 15 dual-purpose MWs, with coach-style seats, delivered in 1958. When all 15 were equipped for OMO in 1968 they lost two seats and were repainted into this livery, having previously been in a variety of combinations of green and cream. EMG356 would finally be withdrawn in 1976. *C. L. Caddy*

As a result of the Mid Wales Motorways takeover the ancient county town of Shrewsbury was served by Crosville for the first time on 15 February 1970. To overcome a shortage of one-man single-deckers a number of OMO vehicles were either hired or purchased during 1967/8, the latter being the first second-hand acquisitions for some 15 years. These included SUG282-91, 10 former Red & White Bristol LS6G/ECW 45-seaters dating 1953/4 and with registrations in the LAX and MAX series. Pictured in the charming surroundings of the independent bus station in Barker Street, with a selection of parcels waiting to be loaded, SUG290 is bound for Criggion, a small village to the west of the town. Payment for parcels traffic was by distance and weight, special tickets being issued by the driver. Widely advertised and well used especially in more-rural areas, the conveyance of parcels and newspapers was, for many years, a useful additional source of revenue. Standing alongside is a Burlingham-bodied Ford 570E belonging to Worthen Motorways. *A. E. Jones*

Above: Mid Wales Motorways was established in 1937 as a co-operative by a number of independent bus operators in the Shropshire area. Its headquarters was in Newtown, 25 miles to the south-west of Shrewsbury. In 1955 it acquired a couple of Crosville's fleet of 21 sturdy Gardner-engined, utility-bodied Guy Arabs (MG137-57) delivered during 1942/3 and assigned throughout their working lives to Crewe depot. Seen during an Omnibus Society visit in the early 1960s, MG156 was a Mk II model with a five-cylinder engine and a Northern Counties body which still retained many of its utility features, although its destination box had been rebuilt in the two-piece Tilling style. Along with sister MG155 it gave a further six years' service with Mid Wales and was 20 years old when sent for scrap. *Peter Roberts*

Right: Why the Crosland-Taylors felt drawn towards establishing loss-making outposts in some of the least-populated parts of Wales is a mystery. One such location was Llanidloes, which from 1924 until 1956 remained in splendid isolation. The original small depot (1925) was replaced in 1950 by new premises but with an increasingly scaled-down staff. Seen at Llanidloes on 20 August 1966 is another of the semi-integral Bristol LSs dating from 1952/3. However, EUG302 is of particular interest. New as UG302, it had received a new 39-seat dual-purpose body in 1957 following an accident and was reclassified the following year when the new system was introduced. In rebuilt form it was to outlast all other Crosville LSs by more than 12 months, not being sold until September 1972. *D. Kerrison*

As a partial replacement for the poorly patronised rail service between Moat Lane Junction and Talyllyn Junction, withdrawn in September 1962, a joint Newtown–Brecon service was introduced, numbered S23 by Crosville and 738 by Western Welsh. This long route, which operated only twice a day, also served Builth Wells and Llanidloes. Dating from 1963, SMG447 was one of the Bristol MW saloons with Cave-Browne-Cave heating, the rather unattractive grille replacing the more characteristic set of wings, and is seen here having just arrived at the Bulwark in Brecon. This scene has now changed: buses no longer terminate or lay over in the Bulwark, the Café Royal Hotel is now the site of Niblett's hardware store, and the Pearl Assurance office is a car spares shop. SMG447 would be among the last MWs to remain in service, being withdrawn in 1980. *G. Morant*

From 1924 the University town of Aberystwyth was one of the southern outposts of Crosville's expanding empire. A 1925 agreement with the GWR defined spheres of influence and limited areas of competition, enabling Crosville to develop a network of local as well as suburban and inter-urban routes, and from 1934 buses were housed in a depot in Park Avenue. To increase the number of OMO-equipped vehicles 41 of the AEC-engined, 35-seat Bristol Ls dating from 1947/8 were rebuilt with forward entrances, driver-operated doors and three-piece destination displays, the top indicator later being painted or panelled over. In this view outside the station the driver of SLA77 has stopped reading his newspaper in order to turn round to issue a ticket, while on the right can be seen one of the familiar system-wide dark-green-on-orange express-stop signs. Ideally suited for working many of Aberystwyth's 'locals', including the S3 to Pwllhobi, SLA77 would be among the last four of its type by the time of its withdrawal in 1967. *G. Lumb*

39

One of the Aberystwyth locals, the S15, served the small resort of Clarach, approached by a very steep hill. In this scene the driver of Lodekka DLB909 has crossed onto the wrong side of the road in order to negotiate a blind hairpin bend on the slow, uphill grind away from the village of Llangorwen. Delivered as ML909 just after the new classification system had been introduced in May 1958, the bus was reclassified as DLB before entering service. Crew-operated double-deckers were allocated to Aberystwyth depot from 1948 until 1970, but DLB would serve with Crosville until 1979. *A. Moyes*

Right: Located on the north side of the Mawddach estuary, Barmouth was developed as a holiday resort during the 19th century. During the period 1953-60 Crosville operated a seasonal 'toastrack' service along the promenade. 'Toastracks' had been introduced by White Rose Motors of Rhyl in the late 1920s, a tradition which Crosville continued, purchasing its last new examples, U12-14, in 1938. Their chassis were built by the Letchworth-based firm of Shelvoke & Drewry. With its small petrol engine (located under the driver's seat), the 'Low Freighter' was more commonly used as a small flat-bed lorry (particularly for dustcarts), but the stylish ECW-built bodies, with eight rows of cross-bench seats, made them perfect vehicles for this sort of service. Withdrawn from Rhyl at the end of the 1950 season, they were eventually redeployed at both Aberystwyth and Barmouth. This view taken at the harbour end of Barmouth promenade in July 1960 shows U12 in its final condition. All three 'racks' had been upgraded in 1955, receiving new radiators and Bedford engines. Watched by a boatman from the Fairbourne ferry, a seasonal conductor straddles the narrow running board ready to collect the fares. A few months later the 'racks' would be withdrawn, and another bit of Crosville 'colour' would disappear. *B. A. Jenkins*

Right: Twenty miles from Barmouth, deep in Snowdonia National Park, was Trawsfynydd nuclear power station. The building of the UK's first generation of such stations was undertaken by Atomic Power Construction (APC), which acquired a number of ex-Crosville buses, among them the former TA9, seen here. To overcome postwar shortages the Tilling Group had purchased a number of Strachans-bodied AEC Regal IIIs, of which a dozen (TA1-12) were allocated to Crosville in 1949/50. In 1955 their bodies were substantially rebuilt, being fitted with rubber-mounted windows, and in 1958 the buses were reclassified and renumbered as SRA901-12. For non-standard vehicles they enjoyed surprisingly long careers with Crosville, finally being withdrawn in 1961/2, at the same time as Bristol Ls of the same age. Unusually for a rare vehicle type in the Crosville fleet, one still survives. After serving with a Territorial Army unit in Colwyn Bay and a spell on a farm in the Conwy Valley SRA905 was rescued for preservation and, superbly restored as TA5, is now in the heritage fleet of Quantock Motor Services in Somerset. *Peter Roberts*

Left: Five miles north-west of Trawsfynydd, on the A487, is Tan-y-Bwlch, which, from 1958 until 1968, was the limit of operation of the restored section of the narrow-gauge Ffestiniog Railway. Opened in 1836, the railway had closed to all traffic in 1946, and sections of the trackbed were flooded by part of the new Tanygrisiau reservoir. Rescued by enthusiasts, it was gradually reopened in stages starting in 1955. A one-way ride on the line was included in various tours and excursions, the return being by coach. Waiting for its passengers in June 1965 was CUG310 of 1953. This was one of the later Bristol LS6G coaches with split (as opposed to roll-down) windscreens. Like others of the batch it had jack-knife doors, sun visors and bus-style front indicators fitted in the late 1950s. In 1967 it was equipped for OMO, and in 1970, a few months before withdrawal, the forward luggage racks were removed. *Alan Mortimer*

Above: Situated 1,000ft above sea level and surrounded by waste from former quarry workings is the town of Blaenau Ffestiniog. Once the epicentre of the Welsh slate industry, it has in more recent years relied heavily on tourism, including organised trips around the one-time quarries for which Crosville had once operated special workers' services. These premises, on North Western Road, had replaced an older depot in the centre of town in 1962 and would be retained until 1990. Peeping out on 12 September 1971 are three Bristol MW saloons and SC4LK SSG671. The somewhat utilitarian buildings, with a small workshop (to the right), appear threatened by the louring mounds of quarry waste, and, indeed, the structure would eventually prove unstable, but the yard is still used today by a local independent. *D. Kerrison*

Left: One of the most spectacular local routes in the Blaenau area was the seasonally operated R40, which from 1964 took visitors up to Stwlan Dam (1,700ft) via a private road, the driver opening the gate with a special key. Later the R40 was revised to include other attractions. The dam itself forms part of the Ffestiniog Pumped Storage Scheme, whereby water is pumped up from the Tanygrisiau reservoir (seen in the background) to Llyn Stwlan off-peak and then used to generate electricity by gravitational flow at busier times. This atmospheric vista, recorded in the early 1970s, features SMG545 tackling the tortuous hairpin bends on its snaking trek up to the mountain road. Skill was required by the driver, as the MW saloons were heavy to steer. With 1-in-8 gradients, the road had a maximum permitted speed of 12mph, and second gear was used in both directions. Unusually, given the overall number of ex-Crosville buses in preservation, no MW saloon has survived.
M. Cozens

Above: Many of the more rural 'heyday' scenes feature a range of OMO-equipped saloons, which the management had hoped would stem mounting losses. However, the unions fought to retain crew operation, and Crosville itself was also concerned for the future of its long-serving employees in areas of high unemployment. Some four miles across the mountains due east of Blaenau was Carrog, served in the early 1970s by the M3 from Llanwrst. Taken over in 1927 from Hugh Jones of Penmachno, the service carried limited local traffic and was retained chiefly to transport people to the National Park. Photographed close to the terminus in 1973 was EMG426, one of a batch of 12 dual-purpose 41-seat MW6Gs (EMG415-26) delivered in 1961. During their lives they wore various combinations of green and cream, this livery of all-over green being the last prior to the imposition of NBC's corporate image; the large lower-case style fleetname dated from 1971. Waiting to pass on this balmy summer's day is a soft-top MGB. *M. Cozens*

Left: Ten miles west of Blaenau is Porthmadog. Located on the Glaslyn estuary, this once played a major role in the export of slate and stone brought to the town by rail. On August 1969 Bristol MW saloon SMG543 of 1965 passes through the resort *en route* to Pwllheli. Historically the R26 incorporated sections of the frequent Blaenau–Porthmadog service established by Crosville in 1924. In this view virtually every house has a TV aerial; like many other operators Crosville suffered from the rapid spread of home entertainment, evening revenue plummeting as people stopped visiting cinemas and other places of entertainment. Another problem was the rise in car ownership, exemplified by the array of postwar British cars of Morris, Ford, Triumph, Austin and Wolseley manufacture. The track of the resurrected Welsh Highland Railway now runs in the road at this point. *A. E. Jones*

Left: Our second view in Porthmadog features DTO588, one of eight all-Leyland PD2s ordered by Cumberland Motor Services but delivered to Crosville (as M583-90) in 1949. These five-bay lowbridge 53-seaters arrived with RM registrations and Cumberland-style front destination displays, of which the two route-number apertures were never used by Crosville. Having spent their entire working lives in Wales, the PD2s would all be withdrawn in 1963. *G. Lumb*

This page: The Victorian obsession with bathing transformed Pwllheli from a small market town and fishing port into a bustling holiday resort served in the season by expresses from as far afield as Liverpool. In the mid-1960s enthusiasts made special trips to Pwllheli to ride and photograph Crosville's first minibuses. Acquired to provide partial replacement for the Caernarfon–Afonwen rail service, withdrawn in 1964, these were a couple of Commer 1500s with Perkins engines and 12-seat bodywork converted for PSV use by Harrington of Hove and were, for a few years, the only non-Bristol/ECW vehicles in the fleet. In the first view, with Pwllheli depot in the background, SCP1 prepares to depart on the R29, which operated Wednesdays and Saturdays only and transcribed a loop through sparsely populated farming communities. In the second view, recorded in October 1968, the little minibus is seen near the village of Llangybi. All too often the only passengers were photographers anxious to find the ideal rustic setting, and an amenable driver would usually agree to pose in some suitable backwater; at other times the photographer simply selected a spot and waited. Following sale in early 1971 SCP1 would see further service with a number of different operators. *Peter Roberts; Alan Mortimer*

Left: The ancient Roman settlement of Caernarfon proved a prime target for Crosville expansion. The first local operator was acquired in 1925, an express service to Birkenhead commenced in 1930, a new depot was built in 1932, and in 1937 an enquiry office opened in Castle Square, where this and the following view were recorded. Both feature the prestigious L1 — the 'Cymru Coastliner'. Inaugurated in 1965 as 'the fast hourly route along the North Wales', this offered a limited-stop service between Caernarfon and Chester, although delays were often encountered, especially at the Llandudno Junction level crossing. Closely identified with the 'Coastliner' were six dual-purpose 50-seat Bristol RELL6Gs — three with curved windscreens and manual gearboxes, and three with flat screens and semi-automatic boxes. One off the latter trio, ERG596 was recorded on 23 June 1967, weeks after it was delivered.
C. L. Caddy

Left: Star of our second view at Castle Square, Caaenarfon, is DFB150, one of the 10 handsome coach-specification FLF6Bs, nicknamed 'White Ladies' by the staff. The provision of coach seats and luggage racks in part of the lower saloon reduced overall seating capacity to just 55 (compared with 70 for the more common bus-seated version). New in 1962/4, the FLF coaches were all originally in this striking livery of cream and black, enhanced by glittering brightwork, but in 1968 they were repainted into the green and cream express livery. Gradually demoted to more mundane work, all 10 would be disposed of by 1977.
G. W. Morant

Seen on the opposite side of Castle Square, CLB255 was in its final weeks in service with a tour party when photographed on 28 July 1965 passing an historic arcade of shops that included Morgan Lloyd's Wine & Spirit Merchants; following a cholera outbreak in 1866, which claimed many lives, several alcohol outlets were established in the belief that strong drink would prevent exposure to the disease. An ECW-bodied Bristol delivered in 1951 (as KW255), CLB255 was one of 39 full-fronted, 30ft-long, forward-entrance, 35-seat coaches, with sliding roofs and six-cylinder 8.1-litre engines, which when new were hailed by Mr Crosland-Taylor as the last word in comfort. They were put to work on the Liverpool–London expresses, but whenever possible they were also employed on prestigious private-hire work, royal openings and shareholders' meetings. Known as 'Queen Marys', all had 8ft-wide bodies; some had narrow chassis, so that the wheels appeared recessed further into the wheel arches, but CLB255 was one of the later vehicles on the wider, 8ft LWL6B chassis. Originally the wings were green, but in 1961 these were painted black to match the rest of the coach fleet. All the 'Queen Marys' were withdrawn between 1963 and 1965, some seeing limited further use, but sadly none of these classic vehicles would survive to be preserved. *G. Lumb*

49

Above: Some seven miles south-east of Caernarfon is Llanberis. Situated at the foot of Snowdon and cradled between Llyn Padarn and Llyn Peris, this one-time mining village has for decades been a magnet for visitors and walkers attracted by the surrounding terrain. It was once the terminus of three railways, all built to different gauges. Since 1896 it has been home to the Snowdon Mountain Railway, and today visitors can also take in the Llanberis Lake Railway. Having just passed the elegant Victoria Hotel, with its acres of garden and woodlands, 1959 Bristol SC4LK SSG628 makes its way along the High Street on service N76 from Bangor via Nant-y-Garth in June 1965. Following withdrawal in 1975 SSG628 would see further employment with Yorkshire Egg Producers, which used it as a staff bus. *Alan Mortimer*

Right: A short distance beyond Llanberis, just before the Pass of Llanberis, is Nant Peris, terminus of the N94 from Caernarfon. This view, recorded on 28 July 1965, features DKA184, one of the initial batch of 22 Bristol Ks, with AEC engines, delivered to Crosville in 1945/6. The original wooden-framed 55-seat lowbridge bodies, built by Strachans to wartime specifications, were replaced in 1953 by metal-framed ECW bodies with standard three-piece destination displays front and rear; at the same time the chassis were overhauled, and new radiators fitted, making these buses virtually indistinguishable from the standard lowbridge Ks. Note than in this view the driver is in his usual uniform, whereas the conductor is wearing a summer jacket. *G. Lumb*

Above left: Having established a strong presence in the university city of Bangor, Crosville rapidly developed it as a starting point for a range of tours and excursions, with a booking office in the town centre. To cater for this trade 47 Bedford OB coaches (SL30-76) were purchased during the period 1949-51. SL77 (EUN 51) was added to the fleet on 1 January 1951, when Crosville acquired the business of Mrs E. Williams of Marchwiel, near Wrexham. Dating from 1947, it became the oldest OB and was photographed at Bangor depot on 28 June 1959. The sturdy OBs, with their 29-seat Duple Vista bodies (some with curved roof glass), allowed good overall visibility and were advertised as 'luxury coaches for private hire', being ideal for 'pleasure tours, sports events, works and church outings, dances, theatre parties, weddings etc — any distance, any number, low rates, reliable service'. In other words anything to bring in the money. During the season the little Bedfords usually earned their keep on private hires and excursions on weekdays and as duplicate expresses at weekends. Intended as stop-gaps and expected to last just six years (although most would achieve at least 10), these were Crosville's last new petrol-engined vehicles and, as such, are fondly remembered for their distinctive engine noise, especially in low gear. Sold at the end of the 1959 season, SL77 would be among several OBs to pass to Vagg's Motors of Knockin Heath, Shropshire. *D. Kerrison*

Left: Spanning the Menai Strait, Thomas Telford's suspension bridge (1826) was altered during World War 2, enabling double-deckers to cross onto Anglesey for the first time; previously lightweight Leyland Cubs had prevailed. The N45 was one of a number of routes which linked the port of Holyhead to the mainland, each via different small towns and villages. In 1962 Lodekka DLB850 was photographed, still with its original three-aperture destination display, on Four Mile Bridge, which connects Holy Island to Anglesey. When it entered service (as ML850) in July 1956 this bus had an open platform, but this was later enclosed. Generally, Lodekkas fitted with Bristol (as opposed to Gardner) engines tended to be disposed of first; DLB850 would be sold to a dealer in 1971, thereafter seeing further service at Ellesmere Port until 1974. *A. Moyes*

Above: At the centre of Anglesey is Llangefni, home to the smallest of the island's three depots, which latterly were grouped together for administrative purposes. Built in 1930, this depot typified the company's cost-effective structures, built with steel frames and sheeting. On the forecourt on 3 March 1971 was CVT682, one of 14 Bedford VAMs delivered in 1967/9. Other than the two Commer minibuses these were the first non-Bristol/ECW vehicles to be delivered since 1951 and reintroduced the Bedford marque following withdrawal of the last OB in 1959. The 14 featured three different body designs, all of which were more common with smaller, independent operators than in the major fleets. CVT682 was one of the first batch of six, which had the early design of Duple Viscount bodywork and the smaller Bedford 330 diesel engine. They were employed principally on tours and excursions but made occasional sorties on other duties. When disposed of at 10/11 years old most found eager second owners, but none is believed to have survived. *A. E. Jones*

Back on the mainland, KA225 stands in Bangor depot yard on 9 June 1958. This was one of 35 Leyland Tiger PS1/1s (KA225-59) with 35-seat Weymann bodies ordered by the Midland General Omnibus Co but diverted to Crosville in 1950. Although they were originally employed as saloons, their stylish design and general level of comfort saw them reassigned in 1952 as dual-purpose vehicles and repainted in coach cream with green waistband and mudguards. The Midland General destination display featured a single blind for the route number and a 'lazy' display for the destination, with a dark glass plate which was flipped over by the conductor to conceal the destination not required; these were later replaced by more conventional equipment. All 35 were reclassified as ETE in 1958 (and had 700 added to their fleet numbers) and then as STE in 1962 after being downgraded once more to saloons. Popular with passengers and crews, these attractive vehicles would be withdrawn *en masse* in 1964, all but one passing for resale to a commercial-vehicle dealer in Salford and three eventually into preservation. Opened in 1931, Bangor depot, the last surviving ex-Crosville depot in north-west Wales, was to close in 2005, and the site has now been cleared. *D. Kerrison*

Situated in the Ogwen Valley five miles inland from Bangor, Bethesa once boasted the world's largest slate quarry (1756), connected to the Menai Strait by means of the narrow-gauge Penrhyn Railway (1801-1962). Seen on the main street, with its impressive three-storey buildings, and having just passed the Purple Motors garage on the left, SSG639 of 1959 was working local shuttle service N71 to Rachub on 17 April 1971. Crosville's 79 Bristol SCs (55 buses, 24 coaches) were always popular with enthusiasts, and at least eight are believed to survive today at varying stages of restoration. *A. E. Jones*

Left: Located 12 miles west of Bethesda, Betws-y-Coed (which translates as Chapel in the Woods) has long been a prime destination for visitors, who arrive today by road and rail to view the town's 15th-century stone bridge, Telford's iron bridge and the Conwy and Swallow waterfalls. Over the years Crosville acquired small batches of new dual-purpose vehicles and also downgraded some former coaches. Their superior interior fittings enabled them to fulfil several functions, including duplication on express services, undertaking private-hire work and operating longer stage-carriage routes deemed worthy of an additional degree of comfort. Parked on the station approach in 1955 was KW168, one of 10 rear-loading Bristol L6Bs (KW165-74) delivered during 1950 with 31 high-backed coach seats (later increased to 32) and which represented the first significant intake of postwar dual-purpose vehicles, the Tigers diverted from Midland General being regarded initially as buses. The express-style bodywork, denoted by additional brightwork and a deeper skirt, was further enhanced by the livery, which also featured a green radiator. The full Tilling destination display was detailing the summer-only service 459. Following withdrawal (as ELB168) and sale in 1962 this example was to see further service with various contractors until 1965. *G. W. Morant*

Left: Downstream from Betws-y-Coed is Llanrwst, meeting point for routes heading south along both banks of the River Conwy. Seen parked outside the depot in September 1967 are representatives of two types long associated with the area. Delivered in 1950 (as KG155), SLG155 was one of the first LL5Gs delivered to Crosville, the longer 30ft body (identified by an extra window bay) allowing four additional seats compared with the early, shorter Ls. New in 1958, CSG623 was another of the SC coaches which had been given a bus-style destination display in 1960 and converted for OMO, with driver-operated doors, in 1966; when this photograph was taken it had just been painted in bus green. SLG155 would be disposed of in November 1967, CSG623 following in 1970 and seeing further use with a Wirral-based scout troop. *G. W. Morant*

Recorded in 1956 from Conwy's 13th-century castle, this panoramic view shows the various structures spanning the tidal Conwy estuary. On the left are the foundations of the long-awaited new bridge (opened 1958), on the right is the impressive Robert Stephenson tubular railway bridge (1846), and in the middle is the graceful Telford suspension bridge (1826). For Crosville this single-lane structure was a formidable obstacle. Stringent weight restrictions precluded the use of double-deckers, the narrow arch at the Conwy end limited the width of single-deckers to 7ft 6in, maximum permitted speed was 5mph, and the annual toll bill was considerable. Only certain types, including prewar Leyland Tigers (as seen here) were assigned to the bridge routes. For many years an alternative had been needed, but by the 1950s the ever-increasing hold-ups were proving detrimental to the economic well-being of the whole coastal area, travellers to/from from Merseyside encountering lengthy delays at the Queensferry and Conwy bridges, the level crossing at Llandudno Junction and on the narrow sections of road west of Conwy. *J. Law / Online Transport Archive*

Also associated with the bridge routes were the unusual and unpopular 'chassisless' Beadle-Leylands. Dating from 1950, these lightweight 35-seaters were of integral construction incorporating radiators, running units and diesel engines from withdrawn prewar Leyland Cubs. Crosland-Taylor recalled that when first they entered service, if the bus was fully loaded with standing passengers, the driver could not release the handbrake unless the standees disembarked, so the body could rise sufficiently on the springs. Although these buses were under-powered and under-braked, in order to maximise the life of the bodies most were fitted during 1953/4 with more powerful Perkins P6 engines and larger brake servos. Latterly they were often one-man operated. When photographed on 12 December 1958 PC30 had just negotiated the narrow arch at the western end of the bridge; described by drivers as 'shooting the wall', this required skill on their part to avoid scraping panels, and it was claimed that one new driver, confronted by the arch, stopped his bus where it was and was never seen again. The unloved PCs were disposed of in 1958/9 following the opening of the new bridge, most going straight for scrap. *D. Kerrison*

The opening of the new bridge on 13 December 1958 led to a revision of services. Most significantly, double-deckers could now pass through Conwy and could thus be assigned to the Liverpool–Caernarfon expresses. The first bus over the bridge was DLG958. Driven by Gordon Jones and carrying civic leaders, it made a special commemorative journey from Conwy to Llandudno. As delivered, the late-1950s incarnation of the LD6G had short mudguards, brightwork above the grille, a shallower (41in as opposed to 48in) upper destination aperture and no opening ventilators in the front upper-deck windows. Following, in normal service on route 412 (Betws-y-Coed–Llandudno), is an L-type half-cab. *D. Kerrison*

This page: During the mid-19th century Llandudno was transformed into North Wales' premier resort, and in the 1930s it also became a major Crosville centre. One terminus was Trinity Square, close to Trinity Church (1874) and the town's main commercial streets, and the location for these two photographs, both taken in August 1957. Between 1936 and 1940 Crosville received batches of Leyland Tigers with a variety of forward-entrance bodywork. Heading the trio in the first view is KA22, one of a batch of 72 TS7s (KA16-87) new in 1937, of which 25 had their 32-seat ECW bodies rebuilt by Crosville in 1950. Although retaining the half-canopy and small destination display they were given rubber-mounted windows (of two different sizes) incorporating sliding ventilators and cream-painted surrounds. On KA22, here working one of the Conwy Bridge routes, the radiator surround has been painted green and the manfacturer's name replaced by that of the operator — both common Crosville practice. Sandwiched between KA22 and a similar rebuild (and seen more clearly in the second view) is KA154; this was one of 12 TS8s (KA154-65) delivered during 1940, all of which retained their original 32-seat ECW bodies, complete with wind-down windows, rain vents and cream flash. To the relief of passengers and crew, all boasted heaters. Long associated with this part of the North Wales coast, KA154 would last until the end of the 1957 season, whilst rebodied KA22 was to soldier on until April 1960, becoming one of the last prewar saloons to remain in service. *A. P. Tatt*

Right: For some 25 years Crosville competed with the Llandudno & Colwyn Bay Electric Railway Co (LCBER) for the lucrative traffic between the two towns, employing its newest buses in attempt to lure passengers away from the trams. In the first of two views ML671, an early (1954) Lodekka, is in original condition, with full-length radiator grille and mudguards, three-piece destination display and cream band running the full circumference of the upper deck. Seen on 17 May 1955, it has just passed one of the ex-Bournemouth open-top cars on Mostyn Broadway, Llandudno. When buses replaced the trams in March 1956 relations with the LCBER deteriorated further. Despite an agreement over schedules, fares and the provision of seasonal 'duplicates' the two operators were constantly in and out of the Traffic Commissioners' court — a situation that prevailed until Crosville purchased the LCBER, for £40,000, in 1961. *R. DeGroote / Online Transport Archive*

Below right: Seen at West Shore, Llandudno, in August 1957, LCBER No 12 (GUF393) was a 1945 Weymann utility-bodied Guy Arab II, which had been acquired from Southdown in 1956. Behind, on route 409 to Rhyl via Colwyn Bay and Abergele, is Crosville ML882, another early LD, new into service that month. Crosville managers and crews must have heaved a sigh of relief when the LCBER buses ceased running in May 1961, as they would no longer have to engage in 'races' to pick up passengers. *A P Tatt*

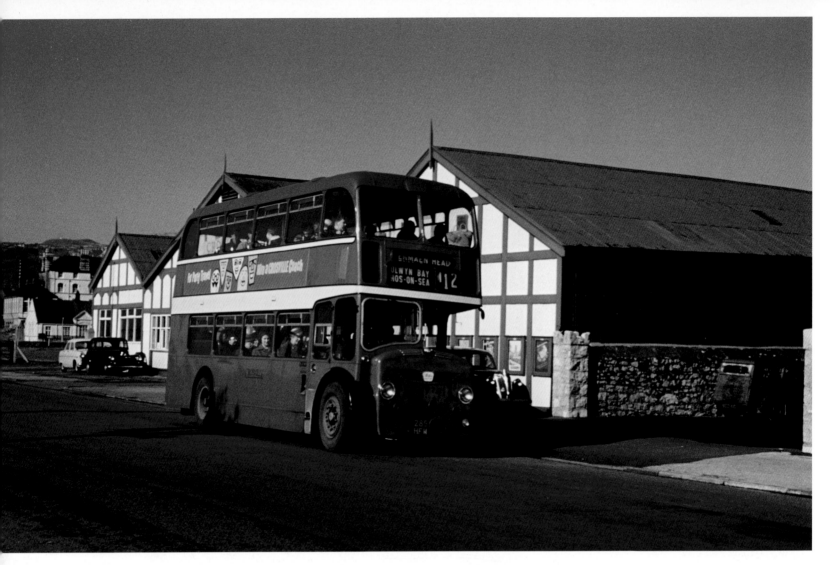

To offset losses at its Welsh depots Crosville relied heavily upon seasonal revenue. During the 1950s, when there was a seasonal19% increase in vehicles, 13% of total annual income was generated between Llandudno and Rhyl, and added to this were receipts from the increasing number of express services to the principal resorts. By 27 February 1960, when this photograph outside the Llandudno Town depot on Mostyn Broadway, the tram tracks had been covered over. Officially a Bristol LDX, DLG949 was the prototype 27ft FS (Flat floor, Short) Lodekka of 1958. All earlier Lodekkas had a slightly sunken gangway downstairs, but this and all examples delivered from mid-1960 had a flat lower-deck floor, air suspension for the rear axles, air brakes (rather than vacuum) and hopper windows, while in place of a conventional radiator grille DLG949 sported a winged Bristol/ECW motif similar to that on many Bristol MWs. This interesting prototype would survive until 1976, but Llandudno Town depot was to close in 1971, its allocation being absorbed by Llandudno Junction. *D. Kerrison*

In 1957 the LCBER tracks at Rhos-on-Sea remained, but the wires had gone. Standing on the front is one of eight convertible Bristol LD6Gs (MG811-8) delivered in 1956 and painted in cream-and-black coach livery. MG814 has the second type of upper-deck railings and a partial perspex screen at the front; the railings occupied the same apertures used to affix the upper-deck roofs, which during the summer months were stored on special racks. The Traffic Commissioners had insisted that Crosville and the LCBER should clearly identify all 'duplicates', hence the destination. On the left is one of the 21-seat Spurling-bodied Bedford OLAZs, owned by Colwyn Bay UDC, which operated from Rhos Pier to Old Colwyn. After acquiring the LCBER in May 1961 Crosville ceased open-top operation at Llandudno at the end of the summer season, but the LD (as DLG814) would remain in service until 1981.
D. Kerrison

A few miles south-west of Old Colwyn is Gwrych Castle, a mock-mediæval mansion dating from the early 19th century. Used to house Jewish refugees during World War 2, it was sold in 1946, and many of the estate's magnificent trees were felled to make room for an amusement park. Known as 'The Showplace of Wales', it attracted 10 million visitors between 1948 and 1968. Pictured running through the grounds on 16 August 1959 is KA5, one of 14 1936-vintage Leyland TS7s given replacement 35-seat rear-entrance bodies during 1949/50 by Saunders Engineering of Anglesey. It was sold for scrap at the end of the 1959 season. For a short time in the early 1960s a service was provided by Rhyl-based open-toppers, but only to the park gates. The estate would close to the public in 1985. *D. Kerrison*

Right: This evocative scene, recorded on 2 September 1964 on the southern fringes of Abergele, features SLG188, a 1950 Bristol LL5G, passing the lodge at the entrance to Bryn Gwenallt Hall, on route M1 from Rhyl to Llanrwst. Originally the bodies on these Bristol Ls had two full-width blinds, the upper one displaying the destination, and the lower the 'via' points and route number; however, to aid interchangability of blinds the display was later panelled over to leave a small route-number aperture above a larger one accommodating a standard-width destination blind. Crosville was one of the biggest operators of the L-type family, examples being in the fleet from 1945 until 1970, and many surviving thereafter as breakdown or other ancillary vehicles, the last being retired in 1976. More than 15 of these buses remain extant, the type having proved popular with preservationists, but sadly this photograph cannot be replicated, a bungalow having been built on the land in the foreground. *B. D. Pyne*

Below right: Anyone familiar with the heyday of travel on the many express services to Colwyn Bay, Llandudno and points west will recall the long-established 10-minute refreshment stop at the Wayside Café, Bodelwyddan. Located on the busy A55, the café was overlooked by the spire of the 'Marble Church'. On 13 July 1968 most of the passengers from CMG414, a 39-seat MW6G coach of 1961, would have been gulping a quick cup of tepid tea before embarking on the final leg of the X6 (Liverpool–Camaes Bay). Working the X4 (Liverpool–Caernarfon) and by now in the later green-and-cream express livery is one of the five FLF6B coaches (DFB109-13) delivered in 1962, while also providing custom for the café are a Southdown Plaxton-bodied Leyland Leopard, a Duple-bodied coach belonging to an independent operator and an MG Magnette Mk IV. This once-famous Crosville landmark is now a Royal British Legion Club. Latterly converted for OMO, fitted with 43 bus seats, repainted green and reclassified as SMG414, the MW would end its career with Crosville in 1976. *D. Kerrison*

65

Left: Once connected to the coast by a steeply graded railway branch line, the village of Dyserth, with its limestone quarry, was where crews on the Rhyl circulars M35 and M36 took their layover. Featured in the first of two views are DTO594/5, from a batch of all-Leyland PD2s delivered in 1949 with 56-seat highbridge bodywork, the 'O' in the fleet number denoting the powerful 9.8-litre Leyland O.600 engine; they served the company until 1962 and 1963 respectively. Here, although about to head off in different directions, both buses show 'Rhyl' as a destination. Neither would ever be fitted with a larger display, route information being provided by boards in the front nearside window; the bus on the right carries a traditional Crosville 'Widd' plate — a paper sign sandwiched between two sheets of celluloid. *Peter Roberts*

Below left: Mixed doubles at Dyserth on 12 July 1964 in the form of LD-type Lodekka DLB825, dating from 1956, and K6A DKA327 of 1949. The latter was among 25 loaned to London Transport to cover a postwar vehicle shortage, working in the capital from March 1949 until April 1950. After withdrawal in 1966 it would be one of three Crosville Ks prepared by Leyland Motors for export to Canada for operation of sightseeing tours at Niagara Falls; later still it would cross the US border, settling in Detroit, but has not been heard of for many years and is presumed scrapped. However, another of the exported trio, DKA337, is a remarkable survivor: still in Canada, it serves in Saskatoon, Saskatchewan, as the 'Bus Stop Refreshments' fast-food outlet. DLB825 would be sold in 1971 to dealer Martin's of Middlewich, purchaser of hundreds of Crosville vehicles over the years, and is believed to have gone straight for scrap. *D. Kerrison*

Crosville's first-ever Lodekka climbs Dyserth Hill on service M31 to Trelogan in August 1964. One of six pre-production models, it had spent a short period on demonstration to Midland General before entering service with Crosville in April 1953 as ML661. An LD6B model, it had a Bristol AVW 8.1-litre engine and a 58-seat, 8ft-wide, 13ft 4in-high body. In contrast to the older 'lowbridge' designs, with sunken gangways and rows of cramped four-abreast seating, the revolutionary Lodekka had pairs of seats flanking a central gangway on both decks. This was achieved by means of a very low chassis frame with drop-centre rear axle. As the gearbox was located immediately behind the forward-mounted engine a rear-facing bench seat for five could be positioned against the front bulkhead. By the time of this photograph DLB661 (as reclassified in 1958) had had its original slatted radiator grille replaced by the more familiar type. Sadly this historic vehicle would be scrapped shortly after withdrawal in 1970. *B. D. Pyne*

Although brasher than Llandudno, Rhyl was popular with holidaymakers, especially from the English industrial heartlands. Attracted by the miles of sandy beaches, thousands poured into the resort during the postwar years by road and rail, staying in hotels or boarding houses or in the many camp and caravan sites dotted along the coast. To capitalise on this holiday trade Crosville purchased special vehicles for the seafront services. Delivered in 1938 were six Leyland TD5 'convertibles' (M71-6); these had 52-seat ECW bodies with detachable roofs that enabled them to perform as ordinary buses out of season. This had proved particular useful during World War 2. After wearing a variety of liveries they were painted in cream with green wings and radiator casing in 1950. Over-prominent Tilling-style destination displays were a later addition, but by the time of this picture, taken on 23 June 1958, M76 was sporting a fixed signwritten board detailing the route. It would be withdrawn later that same year. *D. Kerrison*

Right: Known as Albion Works, the former Brookes Bros maintenance site in Ffynongroew Road, Rhyl, was rebuilt in the early 1950s as a combined workshop and depot. During several visits Dennis Kerrison recorded many images, including close-up studies of older vehicles, many of which owed their longevity to the extensive postwar rebodying programme. JA7 had started life in 1935 as one of a batch of Leyland LT7s (J4-28) with 5.7-litre, four-cylinder diesel engines and Eastern Counties bodies. In 1949 all received replacement 35-seat ECW bodies built to the then standard Tilling design. Those fitted with Gardner engines were reclassified as 'JG', and those with Leyland 8.6-litre engines as 'JA'. All were withdrawn during 1959/60, JA7 going straight for scrap. The Typhoo Tea advert was very common during this period. Parked behind is one of the AEC Regal IIIs described on page 41.

Right: Our second view at Albion Works, recorded on 2 August 1959, shows 'one-off' KA19. During the body-reconstruction programme many of the Leyland TS7s of 1937 were upgraded, but only KA19 emerged as a dual-purpose vehicle with 32 coach-type seats and sliding rear door. Sold in 1960, it would survive until 1963 with contractors.
D. Kerrison

Left: Crescent Road was the other Rhyl site acquired from Brookes Bros. Following a major fire in 1945 the site was redeveloped as a coach station, all day-to-day maintenance of buses transferring to the Albion. On 23 March 1958 ML675 passed the booking office on express service 127. There were three versions of the Liverpool–Caernarfon route. The 127, also known as route A, had two variations — one via the coast road through Prestatyn and Rhyl, the other via the A55 through Holywell and St Asaph, the two meeting up again in Abergele. The 128, route B, went 'over the mountains' through Chester, Corwen and Betws-y-Coed. These services provided a significant part of Crosville's revenue, carrying 500,000 passengers in 1958, and the delights to be viewed *en route* were fully detailed in company-produced guide books costing 6d (2½p). In 1959 they were renumbered as X3-X5. ML675 was one of eight Bristol LD6B coaches (ML675-82) delivered in 1954. ECW had created these semi-luxury vehicles by adapting the standard Lodekka body to include a straight staircase, additional luggage space, platform and offside emergency doors and 52 coach-type seats. Initially there were two tables at the front of the lower saloon together with two pairs of rear-facing seats. Affixed to the bulkhead was a sweet-vending machine. Additional luggage space was provided by removing the inward-facing seats over the nearside rear wheel. By 1958 these vehicles had gained bus-type indicators, an additional three seats and a new dual-purpose livery, complete with green roof which would later give way to cream. *D. Kerrison*

Left: Although plans for a single central bus station in Rhyl never came to fruition, Crosville acquired various properties in the Crescent Road area, some of which were used to accommodate both permanent and temporary staff, while the provision of a rear entrance at the coach station allowed through movements, which eased the seasonal congestion. Often the non-availability of coaches led to other types being pressed into service. Working the X53 (Rhos via Wrexham) on a wet 26 July 1969 was brand-new SLP146, one of a batch of 16 Bristol LH6P lightweight saloons introduced in 1969. Crescent Road continued to serve as a Crosville coach station until the 1970s, thereafter being used to store vehicles, particularly the open-toppers through the winter. With its buildings demolished, the site is now a rather rudimentary car and coach park. *D. Kerrison*

For some 20 years after World War 2 the seasonal allocation at Rhyl depot increased by 50%. Vehicles such as coaches were bought out of store at the beginning of May, whilst additional capacity, usually in the form of double-deckers, was drafted in from other depots. As a result the services on the Rhyl–Llandudno corridor generated 13% of the company's revenue. The High Street bus station proved incapable of handling the increased traffic, so a summer-only terminus was established in the forecourt of

Rhyl station, where DTE535 is seen with a good load for Tywyn in 1959. This was representative of two batches of Leyland PD1As (originally M521-40 and M541-55) delivered during 1947/8 with 53-seat, wooden-framed ECW bodies. The beading that once framed the upper cream band is clearly visible, while the 'E' in 'DTE' denoted a Leyland E181 engine. Following withdrawal in 1960 DTE535 would be sold to A1 Service of Ardrossan and thence in 1965 to a showman in Kirkcaldy. *Peter Roberts*

This animated scene, recorded on 4 September 1964, focuses on the standard postwar saloons. On the left is SLA18, one of the early Bristol L6As with a 7ft 6in-wide chassis, 7.7-litre AEC engine and 35-seat, rear-entrance bodywork, of which 41 were converted for OMO in 1957. However, all too often they were still crew-operated, as appears to be the case here, the conductor (in his beige summer dustcoat) calling the driver forward. By the time of its withdrawal in 1967 SLA18 would have put in 20 years of service. On the right is SLB281, an LL6B new in 1952 with the longer, 39-seat, rear-entrance body on a 7ft 6in chassis. Both are on route M47, which would be axed in 1971 as an economy measure. The overspill terminus at Rhyl station was the seasonal loading-point for all routes serving points west; nowadays the site is occupied by a smaller bus station which serves as the focus for all routes serving the resort. *B. D. Pyne*

DKB643 of 1953 was delivered in the same year as the first Lodekka. Seen carrying a substantial load in July 1964, it has just left Rhyl's overspill bus station and is making the sharp turn from Bodfor Street into Kinmel Street at the start of its run to Colwyn Bay on the M13. One-time seasonal conductor Geoff Smith, who eventually rose to the rank of Senior Casual Hand in the mid-1960s at Llandudno Junction depot, recalls that the M13 and other coastal routes, especially those serving Rhyl, Colwyn Bay, Rhos and Llandudno, were always hard work for the conductor. Covering for regulars taking their holidays, casual staff put in long hours. Geoff remembers one occasion when his Saturday shift finished at 1.00am and, after a few hours 'kipping on the back seat of a coach', he was at work again at 5.30am for the morning 'Mass' service on the M17. He also recalls that some of the older AEC- and Bristol-engined 'lowbridge' double-deckers, which came out only for the summer season, were distinctly past their best. On a steep hill first gear had to be used to pull away. Drivers could risk a 'crash' change into second, or stay in first and risk the engine overheating. The filler cap could be blown off if the securing chain was missing, and there were dents in the bodywork above the radiator as witness. Many of the buses had their seating re-covered in very slippery rexine. One day a lady of ample beam slipped off the end of an upstairs seat as the bus negotiated the adverse camber at the top of Penrhyn Hill. Her hips became so firmly wedged in the footwell along the offside that the fire brigade had to free her with the aid of a couple of packets of butter. *B. D. Pyne*

Left: Supplementing Rhyl's express, inter-urban, suburban and seafront services were its 'locals'. Introduced in 1946, the 448 linked Weaverton Country Club with Brynhedydd. Pictured at Weaverton terminus on 27 September 1958 is M54, believed to be the last Leyland TD5 to operate from Rhyl depot. It was one of a batch of 24 Titans delivered in 1938, their well-constructed 52-seat ECW bodies (complete with heaters) having proved especially durable. The provision of the bulky standard Tilling two-piece front destination display was a later addition. Destined to be sold a few months later, M54 would serve as a contractor's bus until 1961. A similar fate awaited sister vehicle M52, which happily survives today in preservation. *D. Kerrison*

Above: With the season coming to an end, DLG817 — one of the eight LD6G 'convertibles' delivered in 1956 — already had its detachable top deck back *in situ* when photographed on 2 September 1964. During the 1960s the stud of open-toppers gradually fell from favour, although they were hired out as mobile grandstands for events such as the Derby and the Grand National. In the early 1970s DLG817 would also star in a film version of the hit TV series *On the Buses*, and was destined to last until the early 1980s. In this view, recorded at the Grange Road terminus of route M88, the shops are festooned with cigarette advertisements, and the Welsh edition of the *Liverpool Daily Post* is headlining GCE results. *B. D. Pyne*

Above: Five miles east of Rhyl is Prestatyn, another family-orientated resort, and in this view representatives from the Prestatyn holiday camp, in their blue and yellow uniforms, are seen waiting to greet another trainload of holidaymakers and escort them onto veteran saloon KA3. This had started life in 1936 as one of 15 diesel-engined Leyland TS7s (KA1-15) with 32-seat Eastern Counties bodies, but in 1949/50 all but KA11 received new metal-framed 35-seat bodies built by Saunders Engineering. By July 1959, when this photograph was taken, the large destination display had been reduced to a single-line aperture which, on this occasion, was out of use, a board in the lower saloon having to suffice. Being already scheduled for early withdrawal, this was one of scores of older buses to be omitted from the 1958 reclassification. Sold in 1960, it would see further use with a Bolton-based showman until 1965. *B. A. Jenkins*

Above right: Over the years Prestatyn had two basic seafront services. Operated originally by the 'toastracks', the 447 (Beach–Hillside) was latterly the preserve of open-toppers. However, in this 1957 view at Pendre Avenue one of the wartime coaches long associated with the area is deputising for an open-topper, while posing for the camera is conductor Ivor Parry. KA167 was one of a trio of diesel-engined Leyland TS8 coaches (KA166-8) delivered in 1940 with 33-seat Burlingham bodies featuring sliding doors and destination indicators in the nearside canopy face. Following withdrawal in 1958 it would see further service until 1961 with contractors in Cheshire. *D. Kerrison*

Right: For many years this veteran could be seen alongside the main road between Rhyl and Prestatyn, at its junction with Charleston Avenue, close to the popular Ffrith Beach. It represented the variety of lightweight Leyland Cubs acquired for lightly trafficked routes between 1931 and 1937. Registered FM 7443, it had a 20-seat body built by Brush of Loughborough and was originally numbered 716, becoming N33 in the 1935 renumbering scheme; Cubs were classified as 'N' (petrol engine, normal control — with driver behind the engine), 'O' (petrol engine, forward control) or 'P' (diesel engine, normal control). N33 survived the wholesale withdrawal of Cubs in 1949/50 because it served as a mobile control room at the 1949 Llangollen Eisteddfod and subsequently (from 1950 until 1959) as a mobile enquiry office (numbered 64A), in which role it gained the rather imposing 'ENQUIRIES STOP HERE' board on its roof. After sale by Crosville it became an office for builders in Prestatyn and in the late 1960s it was saved by early bus preservationist Tom Hollis, of Queensferry, who did much to prevent interesting vehicles from disappearing for scrap. It is currently in the care of David Moores of Diseworth, who also owns a number of other prewar Crosville vehicles. If and when it is ever restored it would make a wonderful addition to the ranks of buses from the era. *E. J. McWatt / Online Transport Archive*

Opened in 1937, the depot at Flint had been built to reduce dead mileage and to cater for the growing traffic in this predominantly industrial area and was a well-designed structure with accommodation for more than 50 buses. Although it closed in 1981, after many of its industrial routes had ceased following the closure of much of the massive Shotton Steelworks site, the substantial building lasted for many years in industrial use but was recently demolished. Pictured standing on the forecourt in October 1968 is DFB144 of 1964, one of the numerous rear-loading FS-type Lodekkas delivered between 1960 and 1966. Clearly visible in the background is Bristol LS CUG312 of 1953, newly repainted in its final Crosville livery and — if the destination is to be believed — having recently provided vintage transport on the 'Cymru Coastliner'. *A. Mortimer*